The Power of Creating Through Affirmations

Laurie Leah Levine

Published in Australia by Touch for Life

First published in Australia 2014
This edition published 2018
Copyright © Laurie Leah Levine 2018
Cover design, typesetting: Chameleon Print Design
Author photograph by Fuchsia De Lange

Levine, Laurie Leah
The Power of Creating Through Affirmations
ISBN: 978-0-9775066-1-3
pp378

Acknowledgements

I am so grateful to my husband Stan for all his love and support and for this sometimes up and down journey.

I am grateful for my wonderful friends and family.

Thank you to Jenny and Lisa for your feedback with the book. Thank you to Ormé Harris for the copy editing and Luke Harris of Working Type Studio for the design of my book.

A special thank you to all my wonderful spiritual teachers, including Dr. Michael Bernard Beckwith, Louise Hay, Ernest Holmes and Dr. Angelo Pizelo.

I am so grateful for everyone who is a part of our Positive Living Spiritual Centre community in Australia and around the world.

Thank you to the Angels and all the invisible help and support that is always present.

This book is dedicated to

---

*my Mother Sylvia and my Dad Sandy,
who inspire me daily. Thank you for your
unconditional love and support.*

Introduction

Affirmations have been a big part of my life going back many years since first reading a Louise Hay book in the '80s.

I have certainly battled with negative thoughts and beliefs through my life.

What I have learned is that sometimes it can be challenging to change the negative thought patterns and we may need to fake it before we can make it, with a lot of practice and patience. It is also important to change our belief system if we want to create new things and have the affirmations work optimally. We need to believe what we are affirming.

I was drawn to the power and simplicity of affirmations and how I could change my thinking and my life for the better by affirming something that I wanted that was positive rather than focusing on the negative. We do create what we focus on.

I believe that through affirming on a daily basis about being in a loving and supportive relationship I was able to create the wonderful relationship I now have with my husband.

I am so excited to share these affirmations with you.

Many are based on the principles of Law of Attraction and have a spiritual and uplifting nature as well as helping to build self- esteem.

If there are words in the affirmations that do not resonate with you, please feel free to change them to suit your needs.

It is important to not only write and say the affirmations but to feel them. There is one for each day of the year. How you use this book is up to you.

Discover your own way to feel the healing and spiritual power of each affirmation and take in the energy within you.

Remember this is a process and best to do on a daily basis to get the results you desire.

If you can see it and feel it, you can create it.

If you work regularly with these affirmations they have the ability to change your mental patterns and set up a new way of thinking and creating on a daily basis. It is important to become aware of your beliefs and to continually update the ones that no longer support you.

I know that affirmations have certainly helped me to focus my thoughts more positively and to manifest more abundance in my life.

I hope these affirmations help you to heal, change and empower your life.

Wishing you a blessed,
blissful and abundant life

Laurie

Day 1

I am ready to change myself
and my life for the better.

Bring it on.

I am excited for my next adventure.

I know that the best is always taking
place for me and I am open, willing and
available to receive more good.

And so it is

Day 2

Today is a brand new day.

I am open and ready to receive an abundance of love, light, and healing energy from the Angels and my Spirit Guides.

I am feeling good and I am grateful for each moment.

And so it is

$\mathcal{D}ay\,3$

I am ready to create an amazing life
for myself and my loved ones.

All possibilities are open to me now.

I am clear and know what I want.

I deserve to be happy and prosperous.

And so it is

Day 4

I choose empowering thoughts of
health, harmony and wholeness.

I am grateful for every breath and for
the healing power of my body.

I know that my mind and body are
in balance and all is well.

And so it is

Day 5

I love and accept myself for who I am.

I am ready to create more love
and intimacy in my life.

I am a beautiful person inside and out.

I am grateful for all that I have.

And so it is

Day 6

I let go of the need to control my life
and I know that what I do have control
over is my thoughts and actions.

I trust my intuition and I know that it
is always guiding me in the right
direction for a positive outcome.

And so it is

Day 7

I am the only one that can determine
my self worth. It is up to me.

I celebrate who I am and I am
proud of all that I have achieved.

I am confident, happy and successful.

And so it is

Day 8

Today I let go of worrying about things that do not matter and instead I choose to spend time on things that do matter.

I release the worries I have no control over to the Universe.

I take action steps on the things that I can do something about.

And so it is

Day 9

Radiant health flows through my
body and is expressed in every part
of my being.

Each moment I come back to
knowing my own truth.

All is well, and I share this feeling
of balance and harmony with
myself and others.

And so it is

Day 10

I am grateful for all of the success
in my life and celebrate other
people's successes as well.

I know I am manifesting great things
and having fun in the process.

And so it is

Day 11

Today I let my creative juices flow and
spend time doing what I love to do.

I am a creative person with lots
of talents and gifts to offer.

I am proud of all of the ways
that I express myself.

And so it is

Day 12

I am so grateful to have the freedom
to travel, make money, have fun
and do what I enjoy.

I am a powerful creator with Spirit.

I choose positive beliefs and
thoughts that uplift my life.

And so it is

Day 13

I know there are no such things as breakdowns only breakthroughs.

I am open to seeing the blessings in these situations knowing that difficult times are an opportunity to grow and become more my authentic self.

Thank you, Angels, for guiding me and showing me the way.

And so it is

Day 14

Today I step out of what is comfortable and I am ready to have more fun and experience something new and different.

I am open to taking risks and learning new things that empower my life.

And so it is

Day 15

I let go of worrying about how things
are going to manifest or turn out.

I know that this is the job of the Universe.

I courageously take steps forward
with a great deal of trust and
an open mind and heart.

I am grateful for the journey.

And so it is

Day 16

Today I am going to practice
loving people for who they are.

I know the only person that I can
change is me.

I believe that through the power of love
and acceptance all is possible.

And so it is

Day 17

I say yes to love, yes to more intimacy
and romance in my life.

I let my heart be open and allow
wonderful things to flow into my life.

I deserve to be happy and to be loved.

And so it is

Day 18

I let go and release fearful thoughts and
know they have no power over me.

I have control over my thoughts
and my fears.

I remember that I am in charge
of my mind and emotions.

In this moment I feel peaceful.

And so it is

$\mathcal{D}ay$ 19

I am open and willing to forgive myself
for things that have happened.

I know I did the best I could at the time.

There are no mistakes;
only opportunities to learn more
about myself.

I love and accept myself for who I am.

And so it is

Day 20

I am productive, organized and
motivated.

My mind is clear and focused and
I get things done easily.

I enjoy all that I am doing and love
expressing myself and my talents.

And so it is

Day 21

I choose prosperous thoughts and beliefs.

I am open to the wealth of the Universe
manifesting in my life and in my
financial affairs now.

New opportunities to make money
are showing up in the perfect time.

I know that all my needs are met.

And so it is

Day 22

My body has amazing healing abilities.

I take loving care of myself.

Self-care and feeling good are
priorities for me now.

When I feel good I attract more positive
experiences into my life.

And so it is

Day 23

I am so much more than I think I am.

Today, I embrace the
beautiful soul that I am.

I embrace my beauty, divinity,
truth and light.

I am grateful for the person that I am.

And so it is

Day 24

I am creating more peace within me
by forgiving myself and letting
go of the past.

I know my inner world reflects
my outer world.

I breathe in peace and compassion
for myself and others.

And so it is

$\mathcal{D}$ay 25

I am manifesting positive and
supportive people in my life.

My life is good and I am grateful
for this moment in time and all
that I am creating.

I am living my dreams and enjoying
all that I am experiencing.

And so it is

Day 26

I am open and ready to tap into
my inner healer to support my body
in any way I can.

I am listening to the messages my body
is giving me and I am creating
an internal harmonious environment
by my thoughts and actions.

And so it is

Day 27

I trust and know that joy is in the journey
of life and I tap into that joy now.

I say yes to enjoying my life even more
and doing things that make
me feel happy inside.

I am grateful.

And so it is

Day 28

I breathe deeply and know that in
the core of my being I am safe.

I value myself and believe that all is
unfolding for my highest good and for
the highest good of all concerned.

I know that I am always divinely guided,
directed, loved and supported
by Spirit and the Angels.

And so it is

Day 29

I surrender and let go of resistance
knowing that within me are
all the answers, guidance and
love for my life that I will ever need.

I trust in me.

I trust in God.

I trust in life.

And so it is

Day 30

I am grateful for new opportunities and
ventures opening up in my life.
They are exactly what I am ready for.

All that I need is always provided for me.

I am excited about all that is
manifesting for me now.

And so it is

Day 31

I am peaceful and calm.

I believe in myself and trust
the decisions I make.

I am intuitive and always guided
to what I need to do next.

And so it is

Day 32

I release any judgment I have
against myself or others.

I know that my breakdowns are
breakthroughs waiting to happen.

I begin now to love and accept myself
on a deeper level each and every day.

And so it is

Day 33

Today I embrace a whole new way
of experiencing my life.

I choose to have a positive attitude
and outlook. I am seeing the good
in everything and in everyone
I come into contact with.

I have an expanded image of myself
and others.

I know that so much is possible
when I believe.

And so it is

Day 34

It is easy for me to receive love and
compliments from others.

I let go of old and outdated beliefs
about myself and I am open
to great things coming my way.

I am worthy and I accept it all now.

And so it is

Day 35

I take the time today to stop and
smell the roses and appreciate
the beauty that is all around me.

Spending time in nature calms me and
nourishes my body, mind and soul.

I am deserving of all the goodness
and grace that life has to offer.

And so it is

Day 36

Today I am grateful for my life and the wonderful people that I love and that love me.

I appreciate all that has come before this moment.

I know that every challenge has taught me so much and made me a better person.

And so it is

Day 37

I am one with the Divine and I am
a beautiful person inside and out.

I am focused on every day miracles
taking place.

I let go of resistance
and I choose to live my life from
a loving and positive place.

And so it is

Day 38

My life is filled with infinite love
and possibilities.

I am capable of experiencing and
achieving all of my dreams.

I make choices and take my
next steps from this place
of certainty and confidence.

And so it is

Day 39

I give thanks for my wisdom, knowledge
and awareness that I have and
how I trust it more and more.

I let go of any thoughts of lack
or limitation and recognize the full
potential that is within me now.

And so it is

Day 40

Today I take a leap of faith.

Whenever things in my life feel difficult,
I trust and remember how much
the Universe loves me and wants
the best for me.

I surrender to greater peace and
serenity within me.

Thank you, Angels, for all your love
and support.

And so it is

Day 41

I am true to my word and integrity
is a very important value to me.

I know that I attract people in my life
that are also true to their word
and trustworthy.

I have wonderful people in my life
that I can count on.

And so it is

$\mathcal{D}ay$ 42

I have power over my mind.

I am focused on keeping my agreements
and living an abundant and fruitful life.

I know that every thought has a
vibration and I choose high frequency
and prosperous thoughts and beliefs.

And so it is

Day 43

My perception of myself and
what is possible is expanding.

I know that prosperity and abundance
are my natural birthright.

I am abundant and good flows freely
to me in all areas of my life.

And so it is

Day 44

I love to give and I also love to receive.

I am grateful for all that I have
in my life.

I know that I create and manifest
in my life exactly what I believe is so.

I trust in what I can see and
what I cannot see.

And so it is

Day 45

It is easy for me to communicate
my truth with others and speak from
a loving and compassionate place.

I am grateful that I am able to express
what I need to say with ease and grace.

People listen to what I have to say
and I am heard.

And so it is

Day 46

I believe in a higher power within me.

I know there are blessings that come
from every situation and I am open
to experiencing them.

I trust that my faith is so
much greater than my fear.

I am truly grateful.

And so it is

Day 47

I am enough and my love is enough.

I let go of the need to please
others at my own expense.

My priority now is to feel good about
myself and to take care of me.

I am ready to feel lighter and happier.

And so it is

Day 48

I am at peace with what is.

I trust the path that I am on is
the right one for me and know that
my spiritual growth and awareness
is constantly expanding.

I am grateful for my life and
for my soul's journey.

I am enjoying each moment.

And so it is

Day 49

I thank my body and mind for its
healing ability and intelligence.

With each breath I take, my body,
mind and soul are being energized and
filled up with light, blessings
and healing energy.

I am ready to have more fun and
to experience life to the fullest.

And so it is

$\mathcal{D}ay$ 50

I am attracting positive thinking
friends and colleagues into my life.

I know that the people in my life
want the best for me and support me
in staying true to myself.

I feel very blessed.

And so it is

$\mathcal{D}$ay 51

I am attracting a loving
partner/relationship into my life
that is perfect for me.

I am ready to create a healthy, joyful,
intimate and loving relationship
that is for my highest good.

And so it is

Day 52

I know this is a time of new energy on
the planet and doing things differently.

I am aware of ways that I can
continually honor myself, others
and the earth.

I am open to loving and forgiving
myself on a daily basis and expanding
my level of awareness
and consciousness.

And so it is

Day 53

I am grateful to know that I am
responsible for the choices in my life.

I remind myself when I forget this truth.

In this moment, I choose good health,
to feel content and to live
a life filled with love.

And so it is

Day 54

Today I say yes to life.

I say yes to experience more love
and compassion.

I say yes to have more energy
and vitality.

I say yes to feel more prosperous
and abundant.

I say yes to amazing opportunities and
possibilities opening up in my life.

And so it is

Day 55

I trust in the divine rhythm of life.

I let go the need for my life to be hard
and the need to struggle through.

I believe that the Angels are always
loving and guiding me with
whatever I need.

I am ready for more ease, flow,
grace and support in my life now.

And so it is

Day 56

Every day and every moment I have a
choice to choose love over fear.

I choose love.

I choose to focus on loving thoughts
and loving actions toward myself
and others.

I let go and I allow more peace
and serenity in my life.

And so it is

Day 57

I am grateful for the changes in my life.

I know they are opportunities
for growth and new possibilities
opening up in my life.

I embrace all that I am feeling
and know all is unfolding perfectly.

And so it is

Day 58

I choose happiness in this moment
and to accept myself fully.

I see myself in a whole new and
expanded way, just how Spirit sees me.

I am perfect, whole and complete
now and always.

All is good.

And so it is

Day 59

I am ready to be free of doubt,
fear and unhappiness.

I am changing my life for the better
and choose to be happy in this moment.

I am ready and open to experience
more love, joy and bliss.

And so it is

Day 60

I am excited to set clear intentions
for my life.

I know what I want to create and
it is easy to set goals and focus
on enjoying each moment.

I deserve the very best that life
has to offer.

I have clarity, confidence and
I feel good.

And so it is

Day 61

I am worthy.

I am confident.

I am happy to be me.

I am grateful for my courage and
willingness to grow and create
an extraordinary life.

And so it is

Day 62

I am in alignment with God's vision
for my life.

I am open, trusting and receptive
to the miracles unfolding in
my life today and every day.

Thank you, Spirit, for this journey of life.

And so it is

Day 63

I call forth and know the highest is taking place for all of my relationships.

I am ready for more love and intimacy.

I have open and honest communication with others.

And so it is

Day 64

I now let go of all that
no longer serves me.

I live, breathe and have my being
in the oneness of Spirit, knowing that
I am always guided and directed.

Thank you, Angels, for your love
and constant support.

And so it is

Day 65

I am grateful every morning for this
new day and all that is taking place.

I am grateful each night before I go to
bed for all that I have experienced
and all the love and grace
that surrounds me.

And so it is

Day 66

I am discovering more about myself
and know that I am the artist and
director of my life.

I am the one that can
make my life better.

I choose to do things that empower
and support me in feeling good and
in being healthy and happy.

And so it is

Day 67

Today I see the people closest
to me in a positive way.

I see them as whole, happy and healthy.

I visualize them as prosperous and
abundant.

I hold the highest vision and know
the best is taking place for them.

And so it is

Day 68

I give thanks for all the people
that have touched my life.

I know we are all mirrors for each other.

My life has been blessed by the
wonderful people I have known
that have made a difference to me.

And so it is

Day 69

I love my body and am grateful
for each and every part of me.

I am sexy.

I am beautiful inside and out.

I am happy to be me and
to shine my light.

And so it is

Day 70

I surrender to a greater place
of peace within me.

I surrender to a greater experience
of love in my life.

I surrender to more joy and bliss.

I let go of trying and surrender to
my life flowing with ease and grace.

And so it is

Day 71

My mind is focused on
what I want to create.

I feel it, visualize it and know
that it is manifesting in the best
way possible for me.

I am excited that the Universe
has something even better for me
than I could imagine.

And so it is

Day 72

I am a spiritual being.

I am limitless.

I can do, be and have whatever
my heart and soul desires.

My mind, heart, body and soul
are in balance and harmony
with my deepest desires.

I know that my questions are being
answered and all my needs are met.

And so it is

Day 73

I am doing work that I love and
that feeds my heart and soul.

I am abundant doing what makes
me happy and what I am good at.

Money flows easily to me.

I am living a prosperous and joyful life.

And so it is

Day 74

I deserve to be happy and to have
wonderful new experiences in my life.

I am willing to try something new today
and know that everything is possible.

I believe that life can be easy,
fun and enjoyable.

And so it is

Day 75

I am grateful for the messages
that my body gives me.

I know that pain is an important
messenger that I need to listen to.

My body is very wise and
lets me know what it needs.

I take good care and nurture myself
on a regular basis.

And so it is

Day 76

I am intuitive.

I trust and follow my inner guidance
and know that it is
my greatest ally and friend.

My inner voice is always directing me
on the best decision and path for my life.

I am so grateful for my intuition.

And so it is

Day 77

I let go of any resentment that I
may be holding onto from the past.

I consciously choose love over fear
and peace over anger.

I know that no matter what is
showing up right now,
there is something powerful and
beneficial shining through.

I see the blessings all around me.

And so it is

Day 78

Today is a brand new day.

I can achieve whatever I set
my mind to and I am proud of what
I have achieved so far.

It is easy for me to ask for support.

I am ready to manifest
what my heart desires.

And so it is

Day 79

It is okay for me to acknowledge and express grief and loss knowing that it helps to open my heart even more.

I am more alive, loving and free when I can let go and embrace how I am feeling.

And so it is

Day 80

I have natural healing abilities
within me.

I know that my thoughts and actions
can make the greatest difference
in healing, transforming and improving
my life and the life of others.

In this moment I choose thoughts
that are positive and healing.

And so it is

Day 81

There is nothing wrong with me.

I love and accept myself
just the way I am.

Whatever I am feeling is perfect.

It is easy for me to express myself.

I am a confident and loving person.

And so it is

Day 82

I focus today on what is
working in my life.

I am ready to put energy out there to
create things flowing easily for me.

I feel good and ready to begin a brand
new day with unlimited possibilities.

And so it is

Day 83

With joy I begin my day today letting
go of any fear and regrets I may have.

I recognize and appreciate
my inner power and wisdom and
tap into it on a daily basis.

I am grateful for all the spiritual
support, love and guidance I receive.

And so it is

Day 84

I deserve good things in my life.

I am worthy of having loving
relationships, work I enjoy and
I am open to receiving it all now.

My life is abundant.

Thank you, Angels, for your love
and support.

And so it is

Day 85

Any obstacles that may be present
are now dissolved.

I appreciate myself, my abilities
and all my talents.

I am an amazing person.

I am proud of myself.

And so it is

Day 86

I choose to focus my attention
on enjoying this moment.

When my mind wanders to the past or
the future I bring it back to right now.

I am ready to be happy and to live
my life to the fullest.

And so it is

Day 87

Today I celebrate all of
my accomplishments.

I am proud of all I have achieved
so far and I continue daily to realize
my potential.

I believe that everything is possible.

And so it is

Day 88

Today I choose to acknowledge
the beautiful light that shines
within me and let it shine!

I believe in me.

I am grateful for my life and
for all that I have learned.

And so it is

Day 89

I choose today to sing my own song
and to express myself in the most
appropriate way for me.

I let my creative juices flow and
I spend the time nurturing
this creative part of me.

It feels good to let my passion
and creativity flow.

And so it is

Day 90

I make a living doing what I love
and what makes my heart sing.

Money flows easily and abundantly
to me now.

I am open to receiving all the good
that is coming my way.

I deserve to be happy and prosperous.

And so it is

Day 91

I know that as I change my thoughts to more positive ones my life improves.

Each and every day I am more aware of what I am thinking and quickly shift my thoughts to more empowering ones.

I am grateful for my expanding consciousness.

And so it is

Day 92

It is easy for me to meditate,
turn within and connect with
that peaceful place inside me.

I love giving myself this
special time just to be still. It is a
priority in my life and so vital
for my health and wellbeing.

And so it is

Day 93

Life is what I make of it.

I am creating an amazing and loving life
for myself with wonderful people in it.

I am a great role model for others.

I enjoy sharing my loving energy
and light with everyone I meet.

And so it is

Day 94

I let go of the need to be right.

My focus is on feeling good.

I am enough and my love is enough.

In this moment I am happy, peaceful
and content within myself.

And so it is

Day 95

I surround all of those going through
a challenging time with loving energy,
light and prayer.

I hold the highest vision of healing and
know that the best is taking place
for each one of them.

And so it is

Day 96

I breathe in healing light and energy
into each part of my body temple.

My body is profoundly intelligent and
has an amazing ability to heal.

I give thanks and am grateful for my
healthy body and mind.

And so it is

Day 97

I know and have faith that something higher and greater is taking place even if I am not able to see it at this moment.

I let go and I let God in.

I let go and I allow myself to be loved and supported.

And so it is

Day 98

I am generous and give unconditionally.

When I give it fills me up with an
abundance of energy and vibrancy.

It makes me happy to give and
be of service to others.

My life is good.

And so it is

$\mathcal{D}$ay 99

I am a money magnet.

I do work I enjoy and am paid
brilliantly for it.

The people I work with and the
environment I work in are very
supportive and positive.

I love expressing my creativity and
sharing my talents with others.

And so it is

Day 100

Whenever I listen to the news I stay
balanced and peaceful within
my own being.

I release the need to hold onto any
energy that does not support me.

I focus my attention on sending prayers
and loving energy to all those in need.

And so it is

Day 101

When I do not know what else to do,
I turn within and focus my mind on
gratitude, prayer and appreciation.

I am grateful for all that I have
in my life.

I breathe in this wonderful healing
energy into every part of my being.

And so it is

Day 102

It is easy to be kind to a stranger.

Today I choose to make
someone's day special.

I am grateful for the ability to make a
difference to another person's life.

And so it is

Day 103

I take time today to smell the roses and
experience the beauty that is around me.

I stop and breathe deeply and
I feel connected, full of grace and
at one with everything.

I am content and grateful.

And so it is

Day 104

Today I choose to de-clutter my home, car and office space.

I know that by doing so I am allowing more abundant energy and prosperity to flow into my life.

I am clear, focused and motivated.

And so it is

Day 105

It is okay for me to ask for help and
receive assistance from others.

I deserve it and people are
willing to lend a hand.

I am open and I am receiving
what I need in my life right now.

Thank you, Angels.

And so it is

Day 106

I am happy to be me.

Today I share my joy, humor and love with others.

It feels good to share my light and expand my vibration.

I am proud of the person that I am.

And so it is

Day 107

I put myself as a priority in my life.

Each day I spend time nurturing
and taking good care of myself.

I know that I can do more for others
when my cup is full and
I am feeling good.

And so it is

Day 108

Today I am open to see
the God qualities in myself
and in everyone I meet.

We are all connected.

I hold a vision of peace and love in the
hearts of all people and the planet.

And so it is

Day 109

I feel good.

I feel empowered.

I am radiant and full of joy.

I am grateful for this feeling of
peace that is within me right now.

I say yes to feeling happy and
being content.

And so it is

Day 110

My practice in this moment is to be
patient with myself and others.

I am shifting my thoughts from
something being difficult to seeing
it in a whole new and expanded way.

I say yes to things becoming
easier for me in my life.

And so it is

Day 111

I choose empowering thoughts
of health and wholeness.

I see myself as perfect, whole
and complete just the way I am.

I know that everything is possible.

I feel very blessed.

And so it is

Day 112

I am a great giver.

I look for places and opportunities
to give my time, money and energy
to make the greatest difference.

I know that when I give,
so much more comes back to me.

I am grateful for all the
abundance in my life.

And so it is

Day 113

I am ready for all the abundant
new possibilities that are opening
up in all aspects of my life.

I am open to knowledge and
wisdom flowing through me.

I am creating financial freedom and
work that I am passionate about.

And so it is

Day 114

Today I find as many ways as I can
to shine my light and brighten up
my day and someone else's as well.

It feels good to be of service and
make a difference.

I choose to live an amazing life.

And so it is

Day 115

I am a powerful spiritual being
of faith and truth.

I am in charge of my life.

All that I need to know to take the
next steps forward are within me now.

I experience miracles and blessings
today and every day.

Life is good.

And so it is

Day 116

I appreciate who I am.

I am grateful that I have the awareness
and inner knowing to recognize
when to take action, when to rest
and when to renew myself.

I listen to what my body needs
and I am in balance.

And so it is

Day 117

Today is a new day and is an
opportunity to have a fresh start.

I inspire people by being authentic
and doing what makes me happy.

My focus is on being happy, healthy
and feeling good.

And so it is

Day 118

I am so much more than I think I am.

I am one with the Divine.

I am made in the image and
likeness of Spirit.

I release old limiting ideas and open up
to experiencing my magnificence
and to shining my light bright.

And so it is

Day 119

My soul is here for a higher purpose.

I am here to grow, learn, love and
appreciate all that life has to offer.

What I am seeking is seeking me.

Thank you, Angels, for all your
love and support.

And so it is

Day 120

Today no matter what I am doing,
I have an awareness of gratitude.

I learn and grow from all that I do
and enjoy even the mundane tasks
like dusting or ironing.

I appreciate all that I have in my life.

And so it is

Day 121

It is my desire to feel loved.

I am ready to be in a loving relationship.

I am a wonderful person and I am
grateful for all the love that is in my life.

And so it is

Day 122

Today I am doing things that
feed my soul and make me happy.

I love finding ways to express
my creativity and sharing my gifts
with others.

I am inspired.

And so it is

Day 123

I choose to be surprised at
whatever the day brings.

I let myself experience that level of joy,
surprise, wonder and innocence
that I felt as a child.

I enjoy having fun.

And so it is

Day 124

I am willing to experience change
in a whole new way.

I see change as an opportunity for
me to grow and to expand myself.

I feel peaceful knowing this truth.

I have faith knowing that everything
has a divine purpose and plan.

And so it is

Day 125

I am ready to update the old beliefs
I have about myself and my body.

I let go of self-judgment and breathe
in abundant blessings of love and light
to every part of my being.

I love and accept myself
just the way I am.

And so it is

Day 126

Thank you, thank you, Angels,
for this moment.

I feel a deep connection with
my heart and soul.

With each breath I fill myself up
with the energy of gratitude and love.

Feeling grateful is my guiding light for
everything I do and everyone I meet.

And so it is

Day 127

Today, I let go of any regrets
that I may have.

I feel peaceful and accepting about
the way things have turned out.

I am content with my life and
I know that I am blessed.

And so it is

Day 128

I say yes to financial freedom.

Yes to love.

Yes to happiness.

Yes to creativity.

Yes to fun and adventure.

Yes to being passionate and
excited about my life.

And so it is

Day 129

Life is sacred.

Each moment is so precious.

I take several deep breaths and breathe
in loving angelic energy into my body.

I know how loved I am.

I feel my deep connection and
oneness with Spirit.

And so it is

Day 130

I am a good person with a kind heart.

My life matters and I make
a difference just by being me.

I am grateful for my values and
what is important to me.

All is good.

And so it is

Day 131

I am and we are the people that
the world has been waiting for.

I am here to be that higher
consciousness vibration in the world.

I am and we are all connected.

What I do and who I am makes
a difference to the greater good of all.

And so it is

Day 132

Today, I am an activist for change,
for love and for peace on the planet.

I know that for anything to change
I first must change and have those
qualities within myself.

I am ready to be more loving, peaceful
and to be of service to others.

And so it is

Day 133

My consciousness and awareness
are constantly expanding.

I have a strong intention to express
myself on a deeper level.

I want to express the real me and
it is okay for me to be vulnerable.

I feel good about who I am.

And so it is

Day 134

I can, I can, I can do it.

I let go of the need to know how it
will happen and I trust in the process.

I know that anything I set my mind to,
I can achieve, and have fun in the
process as well.

And so it is

Day 135

I know that by focusing on being happy
and healthy, my life improves and I am
a role model for others to live
a joyful and fulfilled life.

My life is changing for the better
and I am grateful.

And so it is

Day 136

I now accept and create harmonious,
supportive and mutually beneficial
relationships in my life.

My life flows effortlessly and
I know my needs are always met.

In this moment I experience inner
peace, happiness and mindfulness.

And so it is

Day 137

Today I take time to look after
my body by stretching, exercising
and eating well.

It is up to me to take good care of
my body temple and to honor myself.

I say yes to feeling good and
having lots of energy.

And so it is

Day 138

I trust in the natural flow and
abundance of the Universe.

I know that I am provided with all that
I need and desire at the perfect time.

I am prosperous and I am grateful.

And so it is

Day 139

I am valued and appreciated for the
work that I do and the person that I am.

Wonderful opportunities and
experiences are manifesting for me now.

I am successful and attracting
great people in my life.

And so it is

Day 140

I eat healthy food that gives my body
nourishment and energy.

I bless the food I eat knowing that it is
nurturing, sustaining and healing
my body, mind and soul.

And so it is

Day 141

I deserve to be treated well and
to be loved and cherished.

I know that I am lovable.

I am confident and accept
myself for who I am.

I am enough!

And so it is

Day 142

I know that as I prosper,
everyone around me prospers.

As I make positive changes within,
things around me change for the better.

I embrace my life and am grateful for
my always expanding consciousness.

And so it is

Day 143

I am in control of my thoughts,
my health, my weight and my wellbeing.

I let go of the thoughts and beliefs
that no longer serve my highest good.

I let go of whatever is
"weighing" me down.

I focus my attention on being happy
and feeling good.

And so it is

Day 144

I am filled with energy, motivation
and vitality to do all I need to and
want to today and every day.

I am ready to take the steps that are
needed to achieve my goals and desires.

And so it is

Day 145

It is easy for me to be in charge
of my finances.

I pay my bills easily and joyfully.

I have everything I need
and so much more.

Money comes from many
different sources and outlets.

All is good.

And so it is

Day 146

I am ready to experience more intimacy,
gentle loving touch and sweetness
in my life now.

I know that building a loving
relationship with myself is the key
to creating a loving relationship
and partnership with another.

And so it is

Day 147

I find wonderful ways to express
my joy like I did when I was younger.

I am a joyful and kind person.

I say yes to having fun
and laughing more.

And so it is

Day 148

I recognize and call forth resources and
connections that support me
in achieving my goals and desires.

I have wonderful people in my life
that want the best for me.

I know that whatever I set my mind
to is achievable.

Thank you, Universe.

And so it is

Day 149

My mind is at peace. It feels good
to stop from my busy life for a moment
and have some inner reflection.

I know that when I am calm and
still I can create more of
what my heart desires.

I am creating a peaceful environment
around me that is quiet, loving and
nurturing for my body, mind and soul.

And so it is

Day 150

I am a talented and creative person.

I love sharing my gifts with others.

It feels wonderful to spend time being
inspired and expressing my originality.

I am so proud of who I am
and all that I have created.

And so it is

Day 151

I am grateful to be so connected
and in harmony with the physical
and spiritual world.

I see it, I feel it and I believe it.

I am tuned in and hearing the messages
from the Angels guiding me on my way.

And so it is

Day 152

I am attracting the perfect partner
into my life.

I feel confident and ready to share
who I am.

I am a loving and kind person.

I accept others as they are,
just as they accept me.

And so it is

Day 153

Every job I do is worthwhile and
part of a higher plan.

I learn and grow from every experience.

My work environment is healthy
and supportive.

I trust that I am always guided to
work I am aligned with that utilizes
my gifts and talents.

And so it is

Day 154

I am ready to overcome negativity
by consciously choosing love.

The more I love, accept and forgive
myself, the happier I feel.

I know that as I focus my thoughts
on love, I attract more love into my life.

And so it is

Day 155

I am an optimistic person and
I know I am on the right path.

I am motivated and inspired to
follow my passion.

I am attracting amazing people
and situations into my life.

I am a success and proud of it.

And so it is

Day 156

It is so good to know
that I am never alone.

I am always connected
to a higher power.

Thank you, God, for your constant
love and support.

I am blessed.

And so it is

Day 157

I love my Spirit.

I am beautiful, bountiful and peaceful.

I look in the mirror and see
my radiant self looking back at me.

I am grateful to experience and
share the light that is within me.

And so it is

Day 158

Today I bless myself, everyone and
everything I come into contact with.

I bless the food that I eat and
the clean water that I drink.

I celebrate all that I have and
all that I am.

And so it is

$\mathcal{D}$ay 159

I remind myself to stop, breathe deeply
and take in peaceful energy inside
every cell in my body and to
let go of stress and tension.

I allow my mind to be still for
a moment and bask in the
healing power of my breath.

I have faith that all is
unfolding perfectly in my life.

And so it is

Day 160

My divine purpose here is
to give and receive love.

I enjoy receiving and giving
compliments and praise.

It feels good to bring a smile
to someone's face and
to acknowledge their beauty.

I am a loving and unique person.

And so it is

Day 161

I am excited for this new day.

I see opportunities even
in the midst of challenges.

I know that there are blessings
that come out of each situation.

I am blessed and grateful for the
people in my life that have been
my greatest teachers. They have taught
me so much about myself.

And so it is

Day 162

I consciously let go of any resistance, fear and doubt I may be feeling right now.

It is okay for me to embrace the unknown and to remember that I am safe, loved, guided and supported.

Thank you, Spirit, for always being there for me.

And so it is

Day 163

I have an abundance of ideas coming to me.

I know these ideas birth brand new opportunities to express myself even more.

I am in the right place, at the perfect time and all is in perfect unfoldment.

It feels good to be in the flow.

And so it is

Day 164

My work, life and relationships
are in balance.

I spend time each day making sure
that my energy is divided equally to
give me a better quality of life.

I have energy and vitality
and I feel good.

And so it is

Day 165

I recognize and acknowledge
whatever I am feeling.

I know that my feelings are not
who I am and are just energy needing
to move.

As I acknowledge and release my
emotions, I feel healthier and more
connected to my heart and soul.

And so it is

Day 166

I know and accept that I am the only
one who can determine my self-worth.

I am worthy.

I am good enough.

I am ready to feel confident,
happy and peaceful inside.

And so it is

Day 167

I am a magnet for attracting wonderful
clients, work and money to me easily
and effortlessly.

I accept a quick and substantial increase
in my financial income now.

My mind is focused on prosperity
and staying positive.

And so it is

Day 168

I celebrate my uniqueness
and originality.

It is good to remember that
I am the only one like me.

I am happy to be authentic and to
inspire others to be who they are.

I am grateful.

And so it is

Day 169

I am responsible and in charge
of my own happiness and wellbeing.

I know that as I forgive myself and
others for things that have happened
in the past, I experience greater joy.

I choose to connect with my inner
happiness and joy today.

And so it is

Day 170

Today I practice staying in
the present moment and
leaving the past in the past.

No matter what is happening I choose
to stay positive and to see the
blessing in every situation.

I use my spiritual power of love,
wisdom and intuition to guide me.

And so it is

Day 171

I am a capable, successful, intelligent,
and all-round amazing person.

It feels good to acknowledge
and to be proud of myself.

I am one of my greatest supporters.

I love and accept myself.

And so it is

Day 172

I know my mind has the power to create a life of joy and bliss or hardship and struggle.

I am creating an abundant, peaceful, rich and loving life for myself and my loved ones.

I am deserving and worthy of good in my life.

And so it is

Day 173

It is okay for me to be wealthy.

I am wealthy in love, joy,
energy and finances.

I accept it all now.

I deserve to be prosperous and happy.

And so it is

Day 174

I rejoice in the beauty of
nature all around me.

I am filled with the healing and
revitalising energy of the earth.

It calms me, supports me, heals me
and fills me with peace.

And so it is

Day 175

Each part of my being – my body, mind,
emotional body and soul – is in perfect
alignment with the whole of me.

I am in balance and harmony with
all aspects of myself and my life.

I feel good and my energy is flowing.

And so it is

Day 176

I am grateful to be me.

Being different is good.

I am a courageous, creative
and talented person.

I know I can create anything
I choose to and have financial security
and enjoyment as well.

And so it is

Day 177

I release any energy that is not mine
or of love and light.

My energy is clear and vibrant.

I am always surrounded and uplifted
by loving, angelic energy.

I breathe in light and love and
I let go of tension and stress.

And so it is

Day 178

I am a person of integrity and purpose.

I deserve to be healthy and happy.

I deserve to have loving relationships.

I deserve to do what I love
and to be prosperous.

Yes, yes, yes; I accept this all now.

And so it is

Day 179

I am in a place of prayer and
stillness within my heart.

I am peaceful and calm.

Each time my mind wanders I breathe
deeply and bring myself back to a place
of peace, connection and tranquillity.

And so it is

Day 180

Today I rejoice in the sweetness of life.

I am open to more joy, love
and beauty in my life now.

I celebrate all the good things taking
place for myself and for others.

I am grateful for the abundance
of resources at my fingertips.

And so it is

Day 181

I am a catalyst for change on the planet.

I facilitate spiritual growth in my life
and in the lives of others.

I am an inspiration and a motivator.

I stand for peace, love and
empowerment now and always.

I do wonderful work on this planet
and I make a difference.

And so it is

Day 182

I choose to lighten up in this moment
and to let go of being so serious.

I invite laughter, fun
and joy into my life.

When I let go, I feel lighter,
calmer and happier within me.

And so it is

Day 183

Today, I see myself as Spirit sees me.

I love, appreciate and accept all the aspects of myself, especially the parts of me I find unlovable.

I am grateful to be able to experience myself in a whole new way.

And so it is

Day 184

I have wonderful friends and support
around me always.

It is safe for me to feel vulnerable
and let people see who I am.

My vulnerability reveals
my inner strength, lightness
of being and authenticity.

And so it is

Day 185

I relax in this moment and with each
breath I take, I let my body and mind
release stress and worry.

I breathe in peace and
breathe out tension.

My mind and body are
feeling lighter and more at ease.

And so it is

Day 186

No matter what others say about me,
I know the truth and I stay balanced.

I let go of reacting and respond from
a place of love for myself and others.

I know I am a wonderful person:
loving, kind and caring.

And so it is

Day 187

I send healing and loving light energy
to all those in need around the world.

We are all connected.

I am grateful for my life, health,
freedom and all that I have.

And so it is

Day 188

I take the time each day to stretch,
exercise and to get healthier.

It is important to take
good care of my body.

I do what makes me happy
and nurtures my body and soul.

All is well.

And so it is

Day 189

I am here to remember who I am.

I am a divine emanation of Spirit.

My essence is love.

When I look in the mirror,
I see beyond appearance
to the beautiful being that I am.

I praise my life.

And so it is

Day 190

Today, in this moment, I release and let go of I can't and claim that I can!

The Universe supports me in taking steps forward and living my dreams.

I am a courageous person and I can do it.

And so it is

Day 191

I trust that the path I am
walking is right for me.

I listen to my own inner guidance
and know that all is good.

I give thanks for this present moment
and for my courage and truth.

And so it is

Day 192

I have all the abilities within me to be a
good leader and to inspire others.

I listen and hear what people
have to say.

I feel good when I can uplift
another person and help them
to feel empowered.

I am proud of who I am.

And so it is

Day 193

I turn within and listen to the messages
that my body is giving me.

I am a building a deeper relationship
with myself from the inside out.

I am ready to tap in to my inner healer
and support my body in any way I can.

And so it is

Day 194

Today I focus my attention
on being of service and
looking for ways to help others.

I am here to experience
the richness of life.

I am grateful for this journey and
adventure of my soul.

I know that when I am of service
to another; it fills me up and
makes my life better.

And so it is

Day 195

I am open, ready and available
for an abundance of love, fun, money
and bliss to flow to me.

I free myself from any beliefs
of financial limitations.

I know that money comes to me
from many different sources.

Thank you, Universe.

And so it is

Day 196

My mind is clear and focused.

It is easy for me to make decisions
that are right for me.

I trust my intuition.

I am true to myself and do
what feels good to me.

My body, mind and spirit are
dancing in harmony together.

All is good.

And so it is

Day 197

Today I hold the highest vision
for myself and for the planet.

I trust that the best outcome
is taking place, no matter
what may be showing up.

I believe there is always something
greater that is manifesting.

And so it is

Day 198

Today no matter what I am doing
I am enjoying each moment
and staying present.

I am in gratitude even when I do tasks
like washing the dishes and
cleaning the house.

I appreciate my life.

And so it is

Day 199

I am filled with grace.

I am filled with light.

I am filled with joy.

My cup is full and
overflowing with love.

I enjoy sharing my light
and loving presence with others.

And so it is

Day 200

I let go of the need to be right
and to control my life.

I know that as I let go of limited
and negative thoughts,
my life becomes better.

I am seeing myself, my relationships
and situations in a new
and positive way.

All is good.

And so it is

Day 201

New opportunities to make money
and do what I enjoy are manifesting
now in the most perfect way.

I am grateful for the journey
I have been on and where I am today.

I feel blessed.

And so it is

Day 202

I have everything I need and
all my needs are fully provided
for by the Universe.

I know that doors are opening for me
at the right time and in a divine way.

I am taking the action steps
that are necessary and I am
also ready to receive.

I trust in the flow of my life.

And so it is

Day 203

I am abundantly supplied
with a great place to live, food on the
table, clothing to wear, work I enjoy
and positive loving people around me.

I am filled with a deep sense
of appreciation for all that is.

And so it is

Day 204

I am a leader and I am good
at motivating people to be
the best that they can be.

My focus today is on
the greater good for all.

I am open and ready to
make a greater difference.

I give thanks for my life and all the
blessings that surround me.

And so it is

Day 205

I know that I am a powerful creator.

I choose now to create a loving,
supportive and healthy relationship
with my ideal partner.

My focus and intention is on having
an open heart and feeling connected
and in balance with all aspects
of myself and my partner.

And so it is

Day 206

It is a priority for me to take
good care of myself.

It is important to take the time to
rest when I need and to get exercise
and eat well.

I know that how I feel on the inside
reflects my outer appearance
and overall wellbeing.

I am committed to being healthy,
happy and vibrant.

And so it is

Day 207

Today I choose to see and do things
as if through the eyes of a child.

I am seeing everything in a new way
today, full of wonderment,
innocence, joy and fun.

I am ready to enjoy my life even more.

And so it is

Day 208

Being a loving and kind person
is very important to me.

I know I am enough and
what I do makes a difference.

I am happy that I have
touched many people's lives.

I am proud of my courage
and loving heart.

And so it is

Day 209

I am ready for my life
to be shaken up for the better.

I say bring on the change.

I am ready for new and wonderful
experiences that enrich my life.

I am ready to meet like-minded people
and to have more fun.

And so it is

Day 210

I take steps to move forward in my life
knowing that I am always guided and
directed by Angels and the Universe.

I leave any fear behind and
know that I am abundant and
tapped into source energy.

Every part of my life
is in divine order now.

And so it is

$\mathcal{D}$ay 211

I feel happy and content just being me.

I am a good person and a loving friend.

I appreciate my life and
all the people in it.

I take great pride in all that I do
and all that I have accomplished.

And so it is

$\mathcal{D}$ay 212

I take responsibility for my actions
and my happiness.

I am in charge of my life and my joy.

I say yes to enjoying myself and
to good energy flowing to me today
and every day.

And so it is

Day 213

Thank you to Mother Earth
for the sunshine and beauty
that is in abundance.

Today is a blessed day and I am
grateful for all of nature: for the ocean,
mountains, trees, flowers and wildlife –
and for the opportunity
to experience it all.

And so it is

Day 214

Today, I remember that I am
so much more than my story.

I am grateful for my journey
of life so far.

I appreciate my inner strength,
courage and beautiful spirit.

I am proud of myself.

And so it is

Day 215

I am grateful for the children in my life.

They remind me of my beauty and
innocence and teach me how to be
in the moment and have fun.

It is good to feel youthful and
to be in touch with my inner child.

And so it is

Day 216

New opportunities are manifesting
for me now to make more money
doing what I love.

I am a wealth magnet.

Abundance is my birthright.

My life flows with grace and joy.

Thank you, Universe, for my blessed life.

And so it is

Day 217

It is my true nature to experience
happiness and contentment.

I let go of the past and whatever may be
holding me back so I can be
more present and grateful.

My life is full of love,
grace and blessings.

And so it is

Day 218

I let go of the need to struggle
and go with the flow.

I have faith and trust in the unknown.

I know that I am always taken care
of and all my needs are met.

My focus is on living life abundantly.

And so it is

Day 219

I am attracting what is in divine
alignment with my soul.

I am doing work I love and am in a
loving and nurturing relationship.

I deserve the very best in my life
and I accept it all now.

And so it is

Day 220

My body is doing whatever
it needs to do to heal.

I thank my lungs for the healing my
body receives with every breath I take.

I feel energized and radiant.

My body is miraculous.

And so it is

Day 221

I know my attitude makes all the
difference with how I am feeling
and responding to situations.

I release and let go of old hurts
from the past.

I stay focused on being loving and
I know that good things are happening
in my life right now.

My heart is filled with love
and forgiveness.

I am grateful for my positive attitude.

And so it is

$\mathcal{D}$ay 222

I feel good about myself.

I am proud of all my achievements.

I can do anything I put my attention to.

I love and appreciate who I am and all
that I have accomplished.

I am an amazing and talented person
with so much to offer.

And so it is

Day 223

I appreciate all ups and downs of life as they teach me so much about myself.

Every step along the path is filled with so many lessons and blessings.

I know that the difficult times have brought me to where I am today and have made me stronger and wiser.

I give thanks for all of it right now.

And so it is

Day 224

As I bring my attention within,
I send light, love and healing energy
to every cell in my body.

I bless each part of myself and
know that I am in alignment
with health and wholeness.

And so it is

Day 225

Through the power of love and
understanding all is possible.

I know that love dissolves fear and
helps me to feel peaceful and
good about myself.

No matter what is happening
I choose to be loving.

And so it is

Day 226

I am grateful for the roof over my head,
clothes to wear, food to eat and
a bed to sleep in.

I appreciate all that I have in my life.

I feel so blessed.

It is my great pleasure to give back and
share my good fortune with others.

And so it is

Day 227

I know that the Angels are
always guiding and supporting me
in so many ways.

I am here to be of service and
make the greatest difference.

I say yes to expansion and
to being the best me I can be.

And so it is

Day 228

I have a wonderful community of
friends who love me for who I am.

I am grateful to feel so
much love surrounding me.

It is easy for me to ask for help
and support when I need it.

I am ready to receive.

And so it is

Day 229

I enjoy following my passion and doing what makes me happy.

I know that when I am happy and feel good I create wonderful opportunities in my life and I have more energy and vitality to do what I love.

And so it is

Day 230

I bless and send love and light
to every cell, organ, system and
gland in my body.

My body temple is magnificent
and knows how to heal itself.

I see every cell vibrantly energized.

I feel good!

And so it is

Day 231

Today I let go of reacting to situations
and instead I focus on the miracles
and blessings in my life.

I look beyond the hardships and see
the grace and healing that is always
taking place in the present moment.

I am grateful for my
positive outlook on life.

And so it is

Day 232

I accept all my qualities and the parts
of myself that I may not always like.

There is no one else like me.

I remember that I am made
in the image and likeness of God.

I am grateful to know this truth
about myself and glad to be unique.

And so it is

$\mathcal{D}$ay 233

I know that no matter what is happening
I stay positive knowing that
I am always loved and supported
by my friends and family.

I feel safe, calm and peaceful.

And so it is

Day 234

I let go of worrying about things
I have no control over and focus on the
positive steps that I can take today.

I appreciate all that I have
accomplished and created in my life.

And so it is

Day 235

Today I am updating my belief system
and changing any old beliefs about
lack and limitation to ones
of possibility and wealth.

I know in my heart and soul
that I am prosperous.

And so it is

Day 236

I eat foods that nourish
my body, mind and soul.

The food I eat gives me energy
and vitality.

I bless my food and know that my body
processes and digests it easily.

I am healthy and I feel good.

And so it is

Day 237

I am creating healthy and supportive
relationships with people
who are positive and
desire the best for me.

I know that I deserve the very best
and will not settle for less.

And so it is

Day 238

When I am feeling down, I focus on doing things that make me feel better.

I trust that within me are the answers, guidance and truth that I am seeking.

I choose to listen on a deeper level and stay open to hear the angelic messages.

And so it is

Day 239

I stop in this moment and take in
all the beautiful sounds, smells
and energy of Mother Earth.

I feel my feet grounded in the earth and
I feel connected, content and at peace.

I feel secure knowing that it is easy for
me to take steps forward in my life.

And so it is

Day 240

My mind is focused on inner peace
and gratitude.

I know when I feel grateful I am
connected back to my heart.

I choose to do things from an open and
loving heart and to be happy now!

And so it is

Day 241

Today I am open and willing to see
the goodness in people and to
let go of judgment.

I am grateful for those that inspire me
to reach for the stars and achieve more.

I do my best to inspire others
by following my dreams and
doing what makes me happy.

And so it is

Day 242

I trust my gut instinct and know that
it guides me to what is best for me.

I believe in myself and know
that I am on the right path.

Each day I get to practice
being patient and compassionate.

I am excited about my life and
what is ahead for me.

And so it is

Day 243

I am focused today on holding
the vision for the highest good
happening for others.

I pray for those suffering from
any kind of illness or hardship
and surround them with light,
love and angelic healing energy.

And so it is

Day 244

I claim today that my intention is
to feel good, to make a difference
and to be happy within myself.

I share my inner happiness
and light with others.

I am grateful for my soul's journey
and all that I have learned
and continue to learn.

And so it is

Day 245

I believe, trust and have faith that all is in perfect unfoldment in my life.

Even if I cannot see how situations are going to turn out, I remember that God and the Universe are looking after the how.

I know that I am attracting all that I need in divine timing and all the answers are provided for me.

And so it is

Day 246

I acknowledge my anger and I am ready
to let go and release old emotional pain.

I forgive myself first and foremost
and I then forgive others.

I am thankful for my experiences,
awareness and inner strength that
have helped me to become the person
that I am today.

And so it is

Day 247

I am grateful for the opportunity
to be mindful.

Whenever my mind wanders, I bring my
attention back to this moment.

I feel more peace, love and clarity
when I am present.

And so it is

Day 248

Today I give myself a gift
of taking time out just for me.

I am worth it.

It is important to look after my
wellbeing and make myself a priority.

I can be there for others when
I have taken care of myself first.

And so it is

Day 249

I am sexy.

I see myself and my body
in a whole new way today.

I let go of my old perceptions and
pictures I have had of myself.

I like what I see and am happy with me.

And so it is

Day 250

I surrender to love, loving me
and loving others more deeply.

I surrender to joy and to
living more fully in this moment.

I surrender to greater peace of mind
and calmness within my being.

I surrender to living a graceful
and abundant life.

And so it is

Day 251

I am happy to know who I am
and to experience my beautiful spirit
that shines so bright.

I am here on a spiritual journey to
express my true essence, which is love.

I am ready to enjoy the ride.

And so it is

Day 252

I let go of the need to be right and
choose to be happy and content instead.

I let go of guilt and shame and know
there is no place for them in my life.

I am so grateful to remember that
I can choose to think and feel differently
each and every moment.

And so it is

Day 253

Today, I choose to create and
to live from a consciousness of
wealth and prosperity.

I am a magnet for money and
financial abundance.

This is my birthright and I am in
vibrational alignment with this truth.

I am grateful for my life and
ready to receive.

And so it is

Day 254

I release any resistance
I may be holding onto.

I am free to be me.

I am free to create what I want.

I am free to love and to be loved.

I am free to make choices that my body,
mind and spirit are aligned with.

And so it is

Day 255

I know it takes practice to make
changes and to be accomplished
at something.

Today, I am practicing becoming
the master of my mind.

I choose new beliefs and thoughts that
support me in being healthy, happy
and confident.

And so it is

Day 256

I am motivated, productive
and organized.

I enjoy getting things done and I am
proud of all I have achieved.

I am passionate about the work I do
and my finances flow abundantly.

Life is good.

And so it is

Day 257

Today I am reminded to never give up.

It is easy for me to take steps forward in my life now and create positive change.

I am ready to have the life I desire and deserve.

I am an amazing person.

And so it is

Day 258

I am grateful for the relationships
and friendships in my life
that feel difficult at times.

I know that they teach me so much
and reveal to me what I need to heal,
forgive and love inside me.

My self-esteem is intact and I feel good.

And so it is

Day 259

I feel empowered sharing
what is important to me.

It is easy for me to express myself.

My practice is to stay positive
no matter what is happening.

I am expressing my truth and
remembering that something higher
and greater is always taking place.

And so it is

Day 260

In this moment I let go
of taking things personally.

I release and let go of any thoughts
or emotions that may be blocking me
from being happy and healthy.

My health and happiness
are most important to me.

With good health I can achieve
all that I am here to do.

And so it is

Day 261

My intention today is to focus my mind
on thoughts that support my life.

With each breath I affirm:

I am peaceful and calm.

I am in balance.

I am receptive.

I am loved and lovable.

And so it is

Day 262

I no longer settle for anything
less than what is best for me.

I accept and deserve the highest good
happening in all aspects of my life
including my health, relationships
and career.

I choose to have more intimacy
and love in my life right now.

And so it is

Day 263

Every area of my life is flowing
with grace and ease.

I am open to more love
and joy in my life.

When I do not know what else to do,
I just keep on believing in love and
accepting who I am and where I am at.

I am in the flow and all is well.

And so it is

Day 264

I am grateful for all of the
abundance I have in my life.

I am a magnet for wealth, love, joy and
new opportunities coming my way.

My life is filled
with wonderful blessings.

And so it is

Day 265

I bless anyone from the past
that I may have had struggles with.

They have been my greatest teachers.

I am grateful to be on this journey
and to have experienced all that
I have in the past and all that
is unfolding in the future.

I am in love with life.

And so it is

Day 266

I trust in the divine plan for my life.

I know that things happen in
Spirit's time and not in my time.

I let go of my own time frame and
embrace the unknown with
excitement and wonder.

I know that all is happening
even better than I could ever imagine.

And so it is

Day 267

I am ready and available for greater love
and intimacy in my life.

I deserve to be loved.

I love myself and feel good
about who I am.

I am a positive and worthwhile person.

And so it is

Day 268

I am changing my life for the better.

I claim the very best for myself now.

I am ready to lighten up
and have more fun.

I let go of any resistance
and complications
and keep things simple.

And so it is

Day 269

I know that the answers to what I am
seeking are within me.

The Universe brings to me the people
and experiences I need for my personal
and spiritual growth.

I am grateful for the people
who have been in my life and
all that I have learned.

And so it is

Day 270

I let go and breathe out any stress
and tension I may be holding in my
body and mind.

I am free, I am grateful
and I am blessed.

My life is flowing with ease, grace
and joy.

All is well.

And so it is

Day 271

Today, I let go and release any judgment
I have against myself or anyone else.

I let the past be in the past and focus on
what is happening right now.

My consciousness of love, forgiveness
and gratitude is expanding every day.

And so it is

Day 272

I am ready to bring more fun, joy
and laughter in my life.

I am expressing my childlike nature
and experiencing more spontaneity.

I allow my joy to be expressed today
and every day.

And so it is

Day 273

I celebrate this new day and all the
miracles that are taking place.

I am open to discovering more about
myself and all that I am capable
of achieving.

Every breath and every moment
creates a new beginning.

I am proud of who I am.

And so it is

Day 274

I love and appreciate my friends.

I know they are there for me.

I am so grateful for the unconditional
love I receive from them.

It is wonderful to have friends
that feel like family.

I feel very blessed indeed.

And so it is

Day 275

I am ready to open my heart to love.

Thank you, Angels, for surrounding me
with loving, positive and
supportive people in my life.

My heart is full and I am happy.

And so it is

Day 276

I welcome and greet this new day
with gratitude and excitement.

I feel positive about what
I am creating in my life.

I am in the flow and all is unfolding
perfectly for me now in every area
of my life.

And so it is

Day 277

I am ready to receive more good
in my life.

I get out of my own way and trust
in the knowing that I am always
in the right place at the perfect time.

New opportunities are opening
up for me to prosper and grow.

And so it is

Day 278

I send love, light, and peaceful energy
out to all in government positions
and right around the world.

I hold a vision for peace on our planet.

I know that peace must first start
within my heart and mind.

I am calm and at peace.

And so it is

Day 279

It feels good to see myself in
a new way and to know that
I am sexy and beautiful.

I appreciate and love my body.

I am grateful for my healthy
and gorgeous body.

I am beautiful inside and out.

And so it is

Day 280

My mind is a powerful creator
and I know that as I believe,
things manifest for me.

I am deserving and worthy
of a happy and abundant life.

Bring it on. I am ready!

And so it is

Day 281

My life is precious.

Each moment counts and I am
enjoying it all; even the ups
and the downs of my life.

I am grateful for my positive attitude
and willingness to grow, appreciate
and love my life even more.

And so it is

Day 282

I treat myself with the same
kindness, patience and love that
I treat others with.

I am my own best friend and
I am proud of who I am and all
that I have achieved.

I love and accept myself.

And so it is

Day 283

I have a beautiful light
that shines inside me.

I remember that I do make
a difference just by being me.

I accept myself and I am proud
of the unique person that I am.

And so it is

Day 284

I am a spiritual person and
appreciate my divine connection.

I attract people in my life that are
loving life and are on a spiritual path.

I am grateful for my life
and everything in it.

And so it is

Day 285

In this moment I slow down, breathe
deeply and allow myself to be still.

I let go of the need to rush around.

I feel calm, peaceful and loved.

And so it is

Day 286

The Universe wants me to
prosper and to feel good.

When I feel good my body is
healthier and I am happier and
feel more connected to all of life.

All aspects of my life are
flowing with ease and grace.

And so it is

Day 287

I choose to make the most of today
and every day.

I practice being present and
I let the past be in the past.

My life is a clean slate and I declare that
this moment is a new beginning for me.

And so it is

Day 288

My mind is focused on loving myself
and loving others unconditionally.

My heart is open and ready to
share the beauty and compassion
that is within me.

I enjoy sharing my loving presence
with everyone I meet.

And so it is

Day 289

It is important to me to be
my magnificent self and
to play big in the world.

I am a capable, confident and
amazing person with many gifts
and talents to offer.

I believe in who I am and proud
of what I have achieved.

And so it is

$\mathcal{D}ay$ 290

I am attracting new experiences
and adventures into my life.

I am ready to meet positive people,
to travel and have more fun.

I know that new opportunities
to make money and do things
I enjoy are manifesting now.

And so it is

Day 291

Today, I revel in the stillness
and beauty that is all around me.

I call forth the experience of peace that
goes beyond human understanding.

My body and mind are in perfect
alignment and in harmony
with the whole of me.

And so it is

$\mathcal{D}$ay 292

In this moment I let go and release
any judgment I may have
about myself or others.

I choose to experience and to see the
beauty and divine perfection in myself
and within each person I come
into contact with.

And so it is

Day 293

No matter what is happening in my life right now, I know that something higher and greater is taking place.

I call forth all the love and support that I need and know it is always there for me.

And so it is

Day 294

Today I honor my soul and
I do what makes me happy.

My heart is open and my joy
is expressed through me in
everything I say and do.

I feel good.

And so it is

Day 295

I am creating an abundance of money
that I can use to go on fabulous holidays
and for anything else I need and want.

Money comes to me from
many different sources.

I am prosperous and deserving.

And so it is

Day 296

I love where I live and I am grateful
for all that I have manifested and
continue to create on a daily basis.

Life is good and I enjoy having
a positive attitude.

Thank you, Angels.

Thank you, Universe.

And so it is

Day 297

I am open to experiencing new adventures in my life that my heart and soul are calling forth.

I let go and release any fears that might be holding me back.

I know that wonderful opportunities are presenting themselves to me now.

And so it is

Day 298

I call forth the highest good
to take place for my relationship.

I know love is always present
no matter what is happening.

I choose to stay in a place of gratitude
and to keep my heart open and loving.

And so it is

Day 299

I am calm and at peace with myself,
my life and all those around me.

I choose to make decisions that feel
good to me and uplift my life.

I know that every decision I make
is perfect and teaches me
whatever I need to learn.

And so it is

Day 300

Today is a new day and I let go
of settling for anything less than
what I truly want.

I deserve to be happy and
to live a wonderful life.

When I am true to myself, I am
a positive role model for others.

And so it is

Day 301

Radiant health and wellness flows
through my body.

All my cells and organs are filled
with healing energy, light and vitality.

I feel good, I feel confident and
I am energized.

And so it is

Day 302

I see beyond appearances.

I recognize the silver lining that is
always present in all situations.

I know that I am always supported
by the Universe.

I am ready for my life to change
for the better.

And so it is

Day 303

I am a patient person.

My intention in this moment and for today is to practice being still and breathing deeply.

Every time I feel stressed I bring my awareness back to my breath.

I experience a deeper sense of peace, gratitude and bliss when I slow down and go within.

And so it is

Day 304

I declare today to be a let go of guilt,
worry and fear day.

I know that these emotions
do not have any power over me.

I am in charge of my own happiness.

I have faith and trust that all is
unfolding at the right time and
in the best possible way for me.

I feel free.

And so it is

Day 305

My mind is focused on feeling peaceful.

When my mind is at peace I feel more
connected to my higher self and Spirit.

I rejoice in this deeper loving
connection with my body, mind
and soul.

And so it is

Day 306

I am making the most of today.

I go with the flow and I follow
the things that feel right for me.

I trust and believe in myself.

I am a confident person.

And so it is

Day 307

I choose today to let go of limitations
and start thinking and creating from an
abundant and prosperous state of mind.

I expect good things in my life.

I am open, ready and
available to receive.

I believe that everything is possible
and I am thriving and successful.

And so it is

Day 308

I remember in this moment to
keep things simple.

I am grateful and thankful to be alive
and to be aware.

I let go of the need to struggle
and create difficulty in my life.

I am ready to move forward
with ease, joy and grace.

And so it is

Day 309

I am unlimited.

I have a clean canvas and I can create whatever it is that I dream and desire.

I feel powerful, clear and focused and I believe that all is possible in my life.

Thank you, Universe, for always guiding me in the right direction.

And so it is

Day 310

New opportunities to experience love
and intimacy are opening up
for me now and I am ready.

I am excited to experience
a deeper love in my life.

I look forward to seeing what
the Universe has in store for me.

I know it is good.

And so it is

Day 311

I am grateful for the
sweetness in my life.

I look around at my home, surroundings
and workplace and I know
how blessed I am.

Today I take action steps and move
forward from a place of appreciation
for everyone and everything.

And so it is

Day 312

I love and adore myself.

I choose to enjoy whatever I am doing
and to see things with
a new perspective.

I keep my mind focused on doing things
that help me to feel happy and joyful.

And so it is

Day 313

I have relationships that are healing,
uplifting and intimate in my life.

The people close to me are very special,
supportive and loving.

They want the best for me and
I know that I deserve just that.

I feel grateful and thankful
in this moment.

And so it is

Day 314

I am loved and adored
by my friends and family.

I am grateful for how much they teach
and inspire me on a daily basis.

My heart is filled with appreciation
and joy.

And so it is

Day 315

I look around and I see beauty everywhere.

I take the time to stop, smell the roses and enjoy the sunsets and rainbows.

I see things today with awe and wonder just like it was the very first time.

I am grateful for it all.

And so it is

Day 316

My body and mind are
in perfect balance and harmony.

My mind holds the picture of peace,
health and vitality and my body
says yes I agree to that.

Everything is possible when I believe.

And so it is

Day 317

I step out of what is comfortable for me.

I am willing to try new things
and to take risks that uplift me
and support my growth.

I say yes to living a full life.

I am proud of the
courageous person that I am.

And so it is

Day 318

I am the dream maker of my life.

It is up to me to make my dreams
and desires come true.

I am in charge of my life and
the choices that I make.

My motto is I can do anything.

And so it is

$\mathcal{D}$ay 319

It is important to put myself first
when I need to look after me.

Self-care is so vital for my health,
wellbeing and happiness.

I choose to feel good.

I do something everyday that
is healing and nurturing for
my body, mind and soul.

And so it is

$\mathcal{D}$ay 320

I see myself and my world from
a positive point of view.

I have a renewed excitement for life.

I am creating new possibilities in my life
from the intention of feeling good.

I am happy to be me.

And so it is

$\mathcal{D}$ay 321

Today I let my creativity flow
by doing things that feed my soul
and make me happy.

New opportunities to make money
and do what I love are
manifesting for me now.

I know that I can achieve
anything I want to do.

And so it is

Day 322

Today I practice saying yes
to living a full life.

I say yes to abundance and prosperity.

I say yes to meeting new people.

I say yes to new experiences
that are fun and uplifting.

I say yes to love and yes
to sharing my joy with others.

And so it is

Day 323

Today I remember to stay focused on gratitude.

I feel better when I am feeling grateful.

I experience more joy and energy when I am in touch with appreciation and gratitude.

My heart is open and I feel more loving.

All is good!

And so it is

Day 324

I have a positive attitude and outlook.

I know and trust that the Universe
wants what is best for me and
always supports me.

I feel passionate about my life.

I have wonderful friends and family
who love me for who I am.

I am blessed.

And so it is

Day 325

I am attracting great clients, work that
I enjoy, financial abundance and new
opportunities into my life.

I believe that I deserve the best.

As I open myself up to greater good
I feel more abundant and grateful.

And so it is

$\mathcal{D}$ay 326

I step fearlessly into today and I have
faith and that everything is working out
in the most perfect way for me now.

I trust myself and I have trust in others.

I know that all is well.

And so it is

Day 327

I am grateful for all of the aspects
of myself as they make up who I am.

I am a unique and happy person.

I know there is no one else like me.

I see myself as perfect, whole
and complete just as I am.

And so it is

Day 328

I am deserving of a wonderful life.

I am ready to experience more fun and happiness now.

I let go of any old beliefs that may be holding me back and I say YES to a new way of life.

And so it is

Day 329

Today I remember just how amazing
I am and how blessed my life is.

I am creating loving, honest and
uplifting relationships with others.

I am courageous, confident and content.

And so it is

$\mathcal{D}$ay 330

I give thanks for Mother Earth and
Grandfather Sky for its beauty and
for life itself.

I am grateful for all the elements:
the sun, water, fire, earth and all the
animals and beings that live here.

I am one with the beauty that
is all around me.

And so it is

Day 331

I know that whatever may be happening in my life right now I have all the love and support that I need.

Wonderful people are there to lend a helping hand.

I trust that all my needs are met.

I let go of reacting and focus on feeling calm and grateful.

And so it is

Day 332

Today I release the need to be critical
and hard on myself.

I choose to feel good and to focus on
being gentle, kind, loving and
accepting of myself.

I am a good person!

And so it is

Day 333

I am a passionate person.

I love experiencing new ways of doing things as well as opportunities to experience more joy, love and everything in between.

I am ready to express who I truly am and to be more authentic and true to myself.

And so it is

Day 334

I am grateful for the simple things
in life.

I appreciate all of my senses and my
ability to see the beauty around me.

I hear the sounds of the birds, leaves
moving in the wind and children
playing and laughing.

I appreciate smelling sweet aromas
and tasting wonderful flavors in food.

And so it is

Day 335

I remember that I am a spiritual being having a human experience.

Whatever challenges may be happening, I remember to stay calm and grateful.

I know this experience allows my soul and being to expand and guide me in the direction that is the highest for me.

I am grateful for the love and support I receive.

And so it is

Day 336

Today is a beautiful day to celebrate
my life.

I remind myself to always come back
to a loving heart even though I may
not always feel that way.

I choose to see things from
a positive point of view.

And so it is

Day 337

Today I send loving thoughts
and healing energy out to people
who are suffering and in pain.

I see the best happening for others.

It feels good to be compassionate
and caring toward other people;
especially those I do not know.

And so it is

Day 338

My focus today is on love, love
and more love.

I open myself to receive
and give more love than ever before.

I know that I deserve to be loved
and that I am lovable.

It is good to remember that
my essence is pure love.

And so it is

Day 339

In this moment I stop, turn within,
breathe deeply and send light and
energy to each organ and cell
in my body.

I see all my organs smiling and happy.

Today I focus on inner happiness
and experience deep peace
and greater health.

My body is in perfect flow.

And so it is

Day 340

I am grateful for all my loved ones who
are no longer here that have made such
a difference in my life and know that
they are always in my heart.

I know that all is unfolding in
the most wonderful way for me.

I am loved and supported.

And so it is

Day 341

I spend time connecting with my inner
child and asking what he or she needs
from me.

I send peaceful and loving energy
to that little child inside me.

I feel more balanced and in harmony
when I connect with that pure part
of me and let myself laugh and
have more fun.

And so it is

Day 342

I take control of my life and know that
magic is happening.

I trust my intuition and know that it
always leads me to what is best for me.

I am happy to listen and follow what my
heart and soul are guiding me to do.

And so it is

Day 343

I remind myself today that I am
the master of my mind and my life.

I know that as I change my thinking
my life changes for the better.

It is good to be aware, awake,
and on a spiritual path.

And so it is

Day 344

I focus on moving forward and
knowing that all is possible.

I let go of the need to give
up when things feel too hard.

I look for the silver lining and know
that something good is unfolding
for me now.

I am open to experiencing
more blessings and to asking
for help when I need it.

And so it is

Day 345

I give thanks for all the wonderful
friends and family in my life that
I love and that love me.

I am grateful for the children in my life
that remind me to be fully present
and enjoy the moment.

I am truly blessed by having these
beautiful souls in my life.

And so it is

Day 346

I acknowledge my willingness to
experience new things and step
out of my normal routine.

I am courageous.

I am proud of how motivated and
committed I am to living a great life.

And so it is

Day 347

I celebrate my success and I celebrate others' successes as well.

I am abundant and attract wonderful opportunities into my life.

I am grateful for all that I have accomplished and achieved.

I look forward to all that the future brings.

And so it is

Day 348

Miracles happen when I have the
courage to let go of fear and trust
that there is a higher purpose and
unfoldment taking place.

I let go of the need to control things
and I know that all is good.

I am held, loved, guided and supported.

And so it is

Day 349

I choose to experience bliss, happiness
and joy in everything I do.

I am in control of how I feel and
I choose to be happy now.

Universe, bring on the bliss.

And so it is

Day 350

Today is a great opportunity to increase
my level of awareness and to trust
myself even more.

I trust in what feels right to me and
in taking appropriate steps forward.

With everything I do today I am more
aware of being the best that I can be
and experiencing more joy.

And so it is

$\mathcal{D}$ay 351

I start this day with a greater sense
of love and acceptance for where
I am and who I am.

I practice daily living in the moment.

I am ready to enjoy my life even more.

I am grateful for my awareness
and higher consciousness.

And so it is

Day 352

I am listening to the messages
my body is giving me in the way
of any discomfort or pain.

I know that the answers are inside
of me and all I need to do is to pay
attention and connect with my body
on a deeper level.

I am creating a loving relationship
with my body and with myself.

And so it is

Day 353

In this moment I stop, breathe deeply
and tune into my heart and soul.

I feel compassion for people and
situations in my life.

When I am compassionate my vibration
and energy levels lift and I feel better.

And so it is

Day 354

Universe, I am employed by you.

Today put me to work; give me opportunities to share my gifts and talents, speak my truth and make the greatest difference.

I am grateful for the abundance in my life.

And so it is

Day 355

In this moment I focus my thoughts
and beliefs on health, wellness
and on feeling good.

When my mind wanders I take
a deep breath and remember that
radiant health flows through
my body and all is well.

And so it is

Day 356

Today I give myself a gift of self-care
and spending time relaxing
and being still.

There is nothing I need to do right now;
only practice being instead of doing.

I let any tension go and I focus more
deeply on my breath and this moment.

And so it is

Day 357

I know that there is no separation
and I release thoughts of limitation.

I claim now that money flows to me
easily from many different sources.

I am paid well and I feel abundant.

I am good at receiving
and my life is bountiful.

And so it is

Day 358

Whatever may be happening in my life,
no matter how hard and challenging
it might feel in the moment, I remember
that there is a higher purpose
and reason for every situation
and experience.

I know that all will be revealed
in the perfect way and time.

And so it is

Day 359

The beauty of nature is extraordinary.

I am connected to all of its abundance.

I give thanks to Great Spirit, Mother
Earth and Grandfather Sky.

I celebrate my life and the blessings
that are all around me.

And so it is

Day 360

Every morning when I wake up and each night before I go to sleep I am aware of all the people and situations for which I am grateful.

I am excited about all of the new connections, opportunities and doors opening up for me.

And so it is

Day 361

I am ready to be the best partner
and friend I can be.

It is important to me to be patient, kind,
and honest, and to live from
a place of integrity.

I am here to be of loving service.
I know that as I give from my heart,
miracles and blessings fill my life.

And so it is

Day 362

I am the artist and director of my life.

My life is truly a masterpiece
in all of its glory.

I am a creative person and I am
dedicated to living the most fulfilled life
I can and being a positive role model
to others.

And so it is

Day 363

I am ready for the opportunity to
express how I feel and to be authentic.

I choose to have the best relationship
with others and I know
that all is possible.

I have the awareness to discover
what is really important to me and
to ask for what I need.

I am happy with who I am.

And so it is

Day 364

Wealth and happiness are my birthright.

I say yes to living an abundant
and prosperous life.

I say yes to experience more love
and joy.

I say yes to good health.

I say yes to a deeper
spiritual connection.

And so it is

Day 365

I am filled with joy in my heart and give
thanks for all of the amazing people,
experiences and blessings in my life.

I experience God's grace all around
me and know that I am safe,
supported and loved.

I choose to live each day from a place
of appreciation and gratitude.

And so it is

About Laurie:

Laurie Leah Levine is an International Speaker and Author of Spiritual Medicine and Blessings of Gratitude.

Laurie's main purpose in life is empowering others to live a happy, healthy and fulfilled life.

She has travelled the world speaking, teaching and sharing her healing techniques and spiritual message with others.

Laurie is one of Australia's most highly regarded healers. She is an emotional intuitive and developer of Emotional Release Point Therapy. Laurie is also a Kundalini yoga and spiritual teacher, Science of Mind Minister and Director of the Positive Living Spiritual Centre.

Laurie offers her healing and spiritual sessions by phone, Skype and in person.

Laurie does talks, media appearances and has had her own column in the West Australian newspaper as well as her own Feel Good radio show.

Contact Laurie now to invite her to speak at your conference, meeting, retreat or festival.

You can contact Laurie at:
laurieleahlevine@gmail.com

Laurie's books and products are available on her websites: **www.laurielevine.com** and **www.positivelivingspiritualcentre.com**

You can find Laurie on facebook under Laurie Levine professional page.